I've been fighting this
war within myself

I've been fighting this war within myself

poetry by Antonio Sanchez-Day

Meadowlark
PRESS
Emporia, Kansas, USA

Meadowlark Press, LLC
meadowlarkbookstore.com

Meadowlark Poetry Press
meadowlarkpoetrypress.com
P.O. Box 333, Emporia, KS 66801

Collected and Edited by Brian Daldorph
with permission and blessing from the family of
Antonio Sanchez-Day.

Cover Design by Maura Halleran
Interior Design by TMS, Meadowlark Press

POETRY / Death, Grief, Loss
POETRY / American / Hispanic American
POETRY / Native American

ISBN: 978-1-956578-33-1
Library of Congress Control Number: 2023931934

Antonio Sanchez-Day
July 21, 1974 - March 5, 2021

Of all my worldly possessions
that I will leave behind
when I expire
my written words
in a book
will cement my legacy
as I take a chance
and put my pain
out there
for the world
to see . . .

Antonio Sanchez-Day
From "Prompted, part one"
p. 141-142

Contents

Poems

I. Hometown: *trying to siphon out the love from the hate*

IV. Transformation: *a second chance of life*

V. Ending: *when it's my time to go I will be ready*

Introduction

For forty-six years, Antonio Sanchez-Day took on life. At the end of "Taking on Life," the title poem of his first book, he wrote about his friend who had just "walked on":

> Until next time, my friend, when our paths
> hopefully cross on that Red road . . . I'll picture
> you at the Sundance, attached to that tree
> pierced through the chest with bone, blowing
> your whistle to the sky, taking on life.

Even though he was often vastly outnumbered by enemies on the outside and by demons on the inside, Antonio took on life. He fought against racism as a boy as one of the few minority students at his high school; fought against family troubles; fought as a street soldier for his gang which was for him the "family" he'd always wanted.

Then he had to fight to simply survive in "The System" as he called it, thirteen years of incarceration in which he often felt himself confined in the "basement of the basement," as he'd tell us.

I met Antonio in 2013 when he was finishing up his prison time, determined to turn his life around. His only weapon against all the enemies lined up against him was his pen, and Antonio wrote brilliantly. How many times did I sit in a classroom with him and experience the response by the class to one of his poems: awed silence, then one brave soul speaking up: *That's how it is, man, you got that*, and everyone in the room nodding, saying, *Yeah, you got that.*

Antonio wrote about the hard times of his life, but he also wrote about the joys of life too, the pleasure of simply walking down Massachusetts Street in Lawrence, Kansas, in good weather, running into friends, greeting a friendly dog or two!

Ronda Miller, poet and former president of the Kansas Authors Club, described meeting Antonio for the first time: "I noticed his humble nature, twinkling eyes, and his kind smile. He seemed at his happiest when he was presenting his poetry. He always went out of his way to assist others, even when he wasn't feeling well. I never heard him complain. He was a gifted man in numerous ways."

Journalist Katherine Dinsdale wrote articles about this remarkable poet for *Lawrence* magazine. She thought of him as "a brave miner, courageously following his pickaxe of a pen into unexcavated darkness. What he uncovered would send weaker men running for the hills. But he sought out and shared for too short a time a holy vein of pure gold."

KU graduate student Ayah Wakkad, who joined the jail writing class as co-instructor, wrote: "Antonio left us too soon! My only condolence is that his impressive collection of poetry, *Taking on Life,* will immortalize him as a gifted Native American poet and storyteller, who challenged his past, present and future. Antonio left us too soon, but the effects of his words remain."

Retired business journalist and writer Mike Hartnett, who'd worked closely with Antonio in the writing class at Douglas County Jail, wrote:

When Antonio was serving his second prison sentence, he decided to turn his life around. He joined a writing group at the jail and found his true calling and passion. This all lead to the publication of his first book, *Taking on Life,* and his work on the Criminal Justice Coordinating Council and his work as co-leader of the Douglas County Jail men's writing class.

Anthony Sanchez-Day was born on 21 July, 1974, in Topeka, Kansas, and died 5 March, 2021, at the University of Kansas Medical Center in Kansas City. He had a number of serious health issues. He graduated from Grand River Academy in Ashtabula, Ohio, and attended Haskell University in Lawrence, Kansas. He was a member of the Prairie Band Potawatomi Nation. He is buried at the Dance Ground Cemetery on the Potawatomi Reservation in Mayetta, Kansas. He leaves behind a son, Ontario, and a daughter, Ana, and many friends he was as close to as family.

One week in the jail writing class, Sherry Gill, Douglas County Jail Programs Director, wrote the following tribute to Antonio, a poem included in Antonio's first book, *Taking on Life:*

What a life you have lived. Your words are beautiful
and they are smooth as pure silk.
You have seen such darkness and tribulation.

Through your writings we have
been given a chance to see
inside you. Your words have such
meaning to me, *I feel them.*

I admire your cultural histories
and enjoy reading your stories.
Your heritage is rife with
solemn spirituality.

As a fellow outcast, my heart is
sad to hear of your body's troubles.
Your mind is clear but your body
is not following suit.
Thinking of you, my friend, wishing you well
on your journey.

After Antonio's funeral, I spoke to his Aunt Margaret and asked her if I could look through the papers he left behind. I was hoping that there would be enough for a second book. I was sure that it's what Antonio would have wanted, for he'd written in his poem "Prompted":

Of all my worldly possessions
that I will leave behind
when I expire
my written words
in a book
will cement my legacy.

His aunt thanked me for asking and said she'd be in touch with me after she and other family members had cleared out his Lawrence apartment.

A few weeks later I had a call from Antonio's step-father, Bob, who told me that he'd gathered all of Antonio's writing into a plastic storage crate. I drove across town to Bob's workshop on the north side of Lawrence to pick it up.

The box contained a stack of files and folders, with Antonio's work neatly arranged, some of it inside individual plastic covers, other papers filed in various collections. There were folders full of the rap songs Antonio had told me that he and a friend had written in prison, page after page filled with excruciatingly neat tiny writing, a lot of it illegible to me. I thought of Antonio like a rapper-monk in his cell, transcribing these songs.

Then there were folders of poetry, some of it I'd seen, some of it already published in his first book, *Taking on Life,* but plenty still to collect into a new file on my computer. After reading through all the papers, I assembled a file of 123 pages of new, unpublished work that I hope will, in Antonio's words, "cement [his] legacy."

I am honored to be trusted by his family to do this work, glad that there's enough writing to make a brilliant second book, deeply saddened that Antonio himself couldn't be here to work on it with me. Or is he here with me in my office as I type this, sitting still and silent as he most often did in class at Douglas County Jail, watchful as always, encouraging me to do this vital work well?

You are still with us, Antonio, in these words and in your works previously published, and in the hearts of those who knew you and loved you for showing us the marvelous transformation you were able to make as you hauled yourself out from the "basement's basement," to sit with judges and give them good advice, to tell us all how it is possible to move beyond trauma and to appreciate the simple joys of being alive.

Brian Daldorph
Lawrence, Kansas

Dana Vásquez

My beloved Anthony, it's with a humble yet, heavy heart that I am afforded this opportunity to say everything that I wasn't able to say to you face-to-face. Time is a precious gift that all of us seem to take for granted. I never was able to say goodbye to you. I couldn't hug you one last time. More importantly, I wasn't able to tell you how much you meant to me. You were not only a big cousin to me—you were my bodyguard, my protector. You always watched out for me, even in adulthood. We had our own bond that only you and I knew and that included, writing. It was our way of expressing ourselves in the one way we knew how to. To see how your writings flourished, I can only imagine the heights you could have reached. Anthony, now your writings can reach the heavens as you are now . . . free. I love you!

Your primita,
Dana

An Aunt's Perspective

Anthony was born two days before my son David. I remember my mother visiting Delores (Anthony's Mother) in the hospital. Delores was already Type II diabetic having a difficult pregnancy and delivery. Anthony came into this world prematurely. But Anthony was a fighter and grew in body and spirit.

His mother's intent was to give him the most comfortable and affordable opportunities which were for the most part what we thought "a normal upbringing." Anthony's direction in life was Anthony's. Had it not been for this direction, we would not have appreciated his natural skill . . . writing. I take solace knowing that Anthony discovered and embraced his writing. He knew he had something that transcended all the pain and anguish his life brought. He achieved his mission, he is at peace now.

Aunt Margaret

By Antonio Sanchez-Day

I write because
I write because...

I am somewhat introverted
with a dose of alexithymia

I write because...

it unclutters my mind
purges the negativity
and replenishes peace
while holding my demons
at bay

I write because...

of self-discovery
and mental freedom

I write because...

I am a testimony
to the power of written word

I've been fighting this war within m...

I've been fighting this
war within myself
a lifelong battle
ensues
feeling at times
like my sanity
seems as

Antonio S.D.

in the shadows of the moon
too close to the sun
with the devil
with death for fun
zed by a bullet
ed by a blade
le enduring a chronic illness
my days
y life makin my bones
just wanna rest them
e fire
e "invictus", unconquered
n I retire

Train wreck of addiction
used to get away
ed to escape
its
spread ahead
aboard this
motive
crazy train
tion unknown
ur baggage
ty, anger, insecurit
baily of room
tickets punched
without caution
rails
landscape
llet
tracks
lls, the bells

I.   Hometown:

trying to siphon out

the love from the hate

my life story (13 years)   By: Antonio Sanchez-Day
   Heres a couple numbers I'm gonna throw at ya. I was born on the 21st day of the 7th month of "74". That makes me 2 years shy of 40. I lost my brother when I was 7 years old, and lost my sister when I was 8. In the 3rd grade at the age of 9, I 1st smoked

Sweat Lodge (Part I)

This is it, the moment of truth, a rite of passage, but not primarily of manhood. Rather, a rite of passage from the physical world into the spiritual. All the preparation and teachings have led up to this point. I am anxious and nervous at the same time. My stomach is tense and I can feel it tighten. My breathing is fast and short and my heartbeat's rapid. I am about to partake in a ceremony that's been practiced by my ancestors for hundreds of years. Now it is my turn to experience this and discover if it is to be part of my life and if I shall carry on the legacy of this practice. I am about to find my inner warrior spirit.

Anticipation and a mild fear of the unknown run through my mind. I prepare my mind for the pain and suffering that awaits, and ready my body to endure the intense heat of the rocks and steam inside the lodge. Today I am about to be reborn.

I write because

By Antonia Sanchez-Oy

I write because...

I am somewhat introverted
with a dose of alexithymia

I write because...

it unclutters my mind
purges the negativity
and replenishes peace
while holding my demons
at bay

I write because...

of self-discovery
and mental freedom

I write because...

I am a testimony
to the power of written word

4

I write because

I write because . . .
I am somewhat introverted
with a dose of alexithymia

I write because . . .
it unclutters my mind
purges the negativity
and replenishes peace
while holding my demons
at bay

I write because . . .
of self-discovery
and mental freedom

I write because . . .
I am a testimony
to the power of the written word

Life

Life means various things to different people. Life means something different to me now than it did 5, 10, 15 years ago . . .

Today life to me is first and foremost a gift. This very day, this very moment as I write these words is a gift, a blessing given to me by my creator. A gift that is to be cherished and treated with love, and kindness.

I view life today as anew, so the wonder of life is always present. I create in my life with joy and abandon, without concern of what others think about my creation. Today I know I have the *choice* of creating hell in my life, or creating beauty and peace. I wake up and am stunned by the beauty of the day be it rain, snow, or sunshine. I drink the morning water, life itself and give thanks. I view the given day as a challenge and an opportunity. A challenge to face whatever situations present themselves to me. Challenges are neither good nor bad, neither a curse nor blessing. They are only what we make of them, depending on what meaning we assign them. The assigned meaning does not alter the content of the situation. Our perception gives the assigned meaning.

Today I choose to view all challenges as an opportunity. An opportunity to be impeccable. To act to the very best of my ability upon whatever knowledge happens to be available to me at any given moment. To live this life with the knowledge that every moment, every act matters. To understand that to believe I have all the time in the world is not only foolish, but also takes away from the appreciation of life. Today I savor life to the fullest, and enjoy every moment of this precious time on this red road. Today I don't need anything or want for nothing but to be happy and to live an impeccable life. Needing, and wanting to have something is just an expression of the egotistical desires of my mind's programming and has nothing to do with my spiritual path.

Today my life is expression of the beauty of my spirit and the Great Spirit. I was once told that life is nothing but a dream, and if I create my life with love, my dream will become a masterpiece of art. This is the power of life.

The power of life is inside *all* of us.

My life story (13 years)

Here's a couple numbers I'm gonna throw at
ya. I was born on the 21st day of the 7th month
of "**74**." That makes me **2** years shy of **40**.
I lost my brother when I was **7** years old,
and lost my sister when I was **8**. In the
3rd grade at the age of **9**, I 1st smoked
marijuana. (It is said a person stops maturing
mentally at whatever age they start smoking
weed. So that makes me a **9**-year-old
emotionally). I was placed in
Alcoholics Anonymous at **10**. When I was **12,**
in the 6th grade, I watched my father die,
2 days after meeting him for the 1st time
after he dedicated himself to **7** years of
sobriety, to be able to see me. At **13** years
old I began therapy. When I was **16**, I
was kicked out of Lawrence High, and ran away
from home. I caught my 1st felony at **18**, **4** years
later at **21**, I received my 2nd strike and was sentenced
to **10** years. (Another stated fact: an individual ceases
to mature emotionally at the age he is incarcerated).
So according to both theories, I am mentally **9**
years old, and emotionally **21**. When I went
through D.O.C. in "**96**," I became **#63803**.

My life story (13 years)   By: Antonio Sanchez-Day

Heres a couple numbers I'm gonna throw at ya. I was born on the 21st day of the 7th month of "74". That makes me 2 years shy of 40. I lost my brother when I was 7 years old, and lost my sister when I was 8. In the 3rd grade at the age of 9, I 1st smoked marijuana. (It is said a person stops maturing mentally at whatever age they start smoking weed.) So that makes me a 9 year old emotionally, (in theory.) I was placed in Alcoholics Anonymous at 10. When I was 12, in the 6th grade I watched my father die, 2 days prior to meeting him for the 1st time after he dedicated himself to 7 years of sobriety, to be able to see me. At 13 years old I began therapy. When I was 16, I was kicked out of Lawence High, and ran away from home. I caught my 1st felony at 18, 4 years later at 21, I recived my 2nd strike and sentenced to 10 years. (Another stated fact: an individual ceases to mature emotionally at the age they are incarcerated)

So according to both theories I am mentally 9 years old, and emotionally 21. When I went through D.O.C in '96', I became #63803

In <u>2006</u>, <u>480</u> cheeseburgers later (cheeseburgers are served for lunch every saturday in kansas prisons) I was released. <u>2</u> months later my mother passed away. Her <u>1</u> and only dying request was that I stop drinking. <u>7</u> years later, I have left that <u>1</u> promise broken, resulting in another <u>3</u> year bid. All that adds up to <u>13</u> years I'll have given the Department of Corrections when this is all over. <u>1</u> day I hope I get it togeather.

In **2006**, **480** cheeseburgers later (cheeseburgers
are served for lunch every Saturday in Kansas prisons)
I was released: **2** months later my mother
passed away. Her **1** and only dying request was
that I stop drinking. **7** years later, I have
left that **1** promise broken, resulting in
another **3**-year bid. All that adds
up to **13** years I'll have given the Department
of Corrections when this is all over. **1** day
I hope to get it together.

wordplay

The meaning of life
to me is
discovering who
I truly am
and living life
to the fullest
under a sky so blue

however,
the anger within
at times makes me
more numb and cold inside

trying to siphon out
the love from
the hate
is why I
still write

I stopped breathing

I stopped believing
when my father
stopped breathing
what's the reason
because
I'm not conceiving
the meaning
searching for a portal
through this pain
trying to abstain
from going insane
devil tried to seduce
me into
tightening the noose
then I opened my eyes to
the truth
started to
turn it around

My hometown

People have different definitions of the word *hometown*.
Some define it as their place of birth or where they grew
up. Others define it as the place where they currently
reside. I personally think of *hometown* as the place I grew
up in: Lawrence, Kansas. Lawrence's most popular
claim to fame is the University of Kansas. Lawrence is
synonymous with KU and Jayhawk basketball. I grew
up here and have seen the town expand significantly
throughout the years. With growth comes inevitable
change. Childhood memories in my hometown are
plentiful.

I call to mind memories of my elementary school, Sunset
Hill. Playing in the town's parks and calling them not by
name but rather by their main attraction, the "train,"
"firetruck" and "rocket ship" park. When the pool
downtown only had three diving boards, two low, and a
high dive. If I couldn't afford to go to the pool, I'd go to
the library to escape the summer heat.

Summertime always held the promise of confetti egg
fights at the fiesta or going to the fair and trying
endlessly to win the biggest stuffed animal for a girl I had
a crush on. I used to go to school skate nights at
fantasyland roller rink and try to win repeatedly at
limbo, for a prize to give to the same brown-eyed girl.

Several afternoons of my youth were spent riding my bike in a vacant field, on 6th and Lawrence Avenue, where Dillons grocery store now sits. By the way, I've been in the new Dillons on Massachusetts Street. I don't like it: bring back the old "dirty" Dillons!

I remember Sunset Drive-in Theater and going to see movies at the Granada, and at the Varsity where friends and I would always sneak upstairs, past the velvet rope and onto the balcony. I relive the memory of watching *Clash of the Titans* at the Cinema Twin, only to be interrupted by a tornado that touched down and ravaged the K-Mart next door. Every winter I would go to the hill by Memorial Stadium and use whatever I could to sled down the immense slope.

My adolescence is also full of memories of my life in my hometown. I bring to mind pumping endless tokens into video games at Lemans. Going up to Lucifers for a good scare. Also feeling sad as I rode along with my cousin in his souped-up Chevy Nova, headed to "the drag" (Clinton Parkway) so he could race for the honor of bragging rights.

I would spend Saturday mornings with friends riding our skateboards at Wescoe Hall, defiant until we were run off by campus cops. (Now, Lawrence has a skate park). After that we would migrate downtown and go look for tapes at Penny Lane Records, or get an *icee* at the diner section in Woolworths. The tan man or hat lady were regular sights in those days.

Now there's Dennis with his mannequins, and the Honk-for-Hemp guy with his free edible hemp seeds.

My first job was climbing steps in Memorial Stadium selling sodas during KU football games. I have yet to watch a men's basketball game at The Phog (Allen Fieldhouse), but I did watch the Harlem Globetrotters there. I also was downtown to witness the celebration of KU's NCAA championship. In my adolescent years I was a regular at Pow Wows at Haskell, as well as a regular at the fry-bread stands.

Reminiscing on my early adult years, I think back on working at my aunt's restaurant (La Familia) and her introducing me to Cesar Chavez when he came in to eat after giving a lecture at KU. I had a newfound appreciation for downtown, the nightlife. I would go see numerous concerts at the several venues: The Bottleneck, Liberty Hall, Jazzhouse and Granada. I used to hitch rides out east of town to catch shows at the Outhouse, before it got TV recognition on Jerry Springer for being what it is now. I recall beginning my pursuit of my college career as a student at Haskell Indian Nations University. While doing so, I learned about my heritage and spirituality.

I left Lawrence for 10 years and upon my return I discovered in amazement that the town had grown immensely. Even the nicknames for the town have changed: *L-town, the L, LK, L-boogie* to name a few. I am leaving town again soon for a couple of years and wonder what changes will be made during my absence.

Despite whatever changes will be made, one thing will still remain the same. Hometown pride and the hometown people. Upon my return, I anticipate receiving my degree from Haskell and making it my alma mater. Adding yet another memory of life in my hometown.

LFK

Breakfast of
biscuits and gravy
at Ladybird Diner
reading *Healing Earthquakes*
with a Lieutenant Dan
at Java Break
a stroll down Mass Street
crimson and blue sprinkled everywhere
Jayhawk pride warms my heart
scribblin' under the sun in
South Park
soothes my soul
a high five from Dennis
puts a smile on my face
chicken tacos from Fuzzy's
fill my belly
buy tickets
for an upcoming show
at the Granada
catch a movie
at Liberty Hall
afterwards a walk home
across the bridge
as the moon glows
illuminating the levee
another lovely day
in the LFK

70/30

Genetics bestowed me
with a pancreas that
does not function normally
I am a Type 1 diabetic
diagnosed at the age
of 16
3 shots daily
in my stomach, arms and legs
of Humilin N 70/30 insulin
and an assortment
of pills
are my daily regimen
I've already experienced
temporary blindness
and an amputation
I know more severe complications
await in my future
until then
70/30
is my lifeline

Easier to be me

Been labeled a weirdo
I like being strange
to hell with pleasing the masses
I'm in my own lane

half potawatomi so I'm teased by full-bloods
half chicano so I'm "not Mexican enough"

I love hip-hop, oldies, and heavy metal
and due to the latter, people think I'm into the devil

yeah, him and I have danced a couple of times
mostly during my 13 years behind enemy lines

So lessons learned, behind trying to be what
they want me to be
forget being fake
it's easier to be me

Phantom feelings

Our love was once
strong, vibrant, trusting and true.
It was a healthy love.
Then came the toxic infection
of lies
which lead to the inflammation
of deceit
and rapidly progressed
into full blown betrayal
as the gangrene of vengeance and hate
settled in my heart
my only recourse
was to amputate you
from my life and soul
cut off all feeling
hopefully going numb
ceasing the excruciating pain
that consumed me within.
Before I suffered total loss
of any capability
to ever love again.
Months after the removal procedure
in which emotions were cauterized
I experience brief episodes
of sensory response,
the phantom feelings . . .
I *still* see you
frequent glimpses of you
in my peripheral view
standing next to me
only to have the vision

of you vanish
in the blink of an eye
I *still* smell the scent
of your perfume
and catch traces
of the floral fragrance
of your hair
I *still* savor remnants
of your flavored kisses
and can taste
the sweet nectar
of your arousal
I *still* hear your voice
calling my name
the echo of your laughter
vibrates in my ears
as do your gentle whispers
and heavy moans
of when you were engulfed
in ecstasy
I *still* sense your touch,
the smooth texture
of your soft skin,
I can feel your warm embrace
and your body lying next to mine.
As your scars heal
in this process of rehabilitation
I push forward
with all strength
and determination
to one day
love again

My Grandfather

My Grandfather's name
is *MISHO* (mee-sho),
Grandfather Sky.
At the rising of each sun
I face the East
sing a morning song
and give thanks for
the arrival of a new day
I burn cedar and sweetgrass
and send my prayers with
the smoke as it travels upward
in his direction.
I offer tobacco
to his daughter
my mother Earth
and give thanks for all my relations
the four-legged ones, the winged ones,
the tree people, the rock elders
and the fish clan.
I am the first-born and only son
of my father.
My color is blue.
I am of the thunder-clan
and belong to the big drum
and *MISHO* is
my Grandfather Sky.

I really like this

Sunshine on my face
coffee in my mug
Don Miguel Ruiz in my heart
Santiago Baca in my spirit
Otis Redding in my soul
a gentle breeze at my back
with my future in sight

Retribution

Seeking retribution
from a judgmental society
trying to find my place
in this condescending world
denied by my own kind
not fluent in Spanish
so I'm not a "real Mexican"
not a full blood
so I'm not a "real native"
a social pariah
due to my criminal past
judged because of my tattoos
profiled for the color of my skin
am I not God's creation
just as you?

I am only trying to belong

Divulgence

aggravation manifests within
an irritation of my conscience
provoked by a condescending society
persecuted for actions
governed by counterfeit beliefs
my appearance judged
by superficial narcissists
condemned with stones
cast by hypocrites
a silent rage seeps
through cracks in my soul
like
  sap
    dripping
      from a
        tapped
          tree

only to be scared by truth
and sobered by reality

Prayer

Grant me serenity
to accept the things
I cannot change
set me free
from these chains
of shame
at what I became
I will spare the names
even though they're
to blame
for sparkin' the flame

like the bastard
who stole my innocence
at an early age
and provided the spark
of this internal rage
unleashing demons
from their cage
cursing me with
a family secret
I take to my grave
branding me to be
forever misconstrued
there's a special
place in hell
for people like you

With these eyes

with these eyes
I have witnessed
the evil men do

with these eyes
I have stared
down fear

with these eyes
I watched
my father die

with these eyes
I lost sight
blinded by anger

with these eyes
some appear transparent

with these eyes
the beauty of
life has blessed

Pain don't hurt the same

There's levels
to this pain
'cause all pain
don't hurt the same
lend me your ear
as I explain
there's scars and tattoos
which I've known
to have a few
there's testimonies
to the shit in my life
I've been through
both created through pain
healed and transformed into art
then there are tribulations
in affairs of the heart
in which lies, deceit and betrayal
all play a part
this type of anguish
runs deeper than the flesh
this parasitic torment
will eat you from the inside
I must confess
Oh and don't forget
the long-lasting lingering
suffering of regret
all I've mentioned hurt
yet are mild

compared to the emptiness
created by the separation
of a father
and child

forever more

Bleed unto me your
anguish
let me absorb your
transgressions
cry on my broad
shoulders
anoint me in your
tears
Whisper in my ear your
deepest fears
consume all my joy
in an exchange for a
transfer of energy
my suffering is a conduit
for your happiness
I am yours forever more

I've been fighting this war within myself

I've been fighting this
war within myself
a lifelong battle
ensues
feeling at times
like my sanity
serves as
collateral damage
traumatized
thoughts
night terrors
reclusive tendencies
all after effects
of the conflict within
trust, happiness,
peace, and love
are the unfortunate
and the casualties
of this war

Apr 2

In my
I was
to pa
today
don't
disap
bee
na
f
t

By A

Self-imprisoned (my only fear)
Locked in a cage
at the age of 18
eventually consumed by rage
over a quarter of
a century later
and no out date
he let the anger within
dictate his fate
family and friends
evaporated through time
bonds created

II. Sickness:

I've been fighting this

war within myself

Sweat Lodge (Part II)

The current environment I reside in is Norton Correctional Facility, a medium security prison in the northwestern region of Kansas. In this particular environment, I am only known as Day #63803. I am a 25-year-old male of half Mexican-American descent, and half proud member of the Prairie Band of the Potawatomi Nation. My father is where I get the Native American ancestry from. When he and my mother divorced, I was only 2 years old and I lost contact with my father. I was raised by my mother, a devout Catholic with solid religious beliefs. Growing up, I always wondered about my Native American culture. With no ties to my father's side of the family, all possible connections to my culture were cut off. After coming to prison, I seen the Native group and became interested, so I joined. So here I stand on this day about to learn who I am spiritually and what lies in me beneath the earthly flesh. I shall unveil my true spirit.

It is a brisk Spring morning, the sun is peeking through the clouds that float across the horizon, emitting a soft pink glow, causing a peaceful calm to soothe my anxiety. The members of the Native American Culture Group and I are all gathered at the grounds where we are permitted to practice this sacred ceremony.

The grounds are a wooded area in the eastern outermost perimeter of the prison compound. It is a territory set aside only for the sweat lodge ceremony and pow-wow seasonal dances. It was told to me that an actual medicine man was brought in to bless the grounds when it was first established, thus making the ground itself sacred.

The area stands out from the rest of the concrete structures and the wall-like fence that surrounds the whole prison. Inside of a place that houses all of modern society's outcasts and a place that's also known to breed hate, anger, isolation and violence, stands a little territory of sacredness, humility, peace and tranquility. It's a region that's approximately the size of the infield of a softball diamond encompassed by towering oak and pine trees.

Within the center of this area sits the *Inipi*, a dome-like frame structure constructed of willow branches that stands about five feet in height, and approximately nine feet wide at the base. In the middle of this structure rests a deep stone pit dug into the earth's floor. The structure can accommodate about ten to twelve men to sit around the pit in the center. The frame to the *Inipi* has an arc-like opening facing the east (in Native American beliefs, that's the direction in which all things begin), through which men enter and exit the lodge during the ceremony. From the opening of the lodge there's a path lined on both sides that extends about 10 feet to emerge into a huge pit with its eastern wall built from various sized rocks and stones carefully arranged. This is called the fire pit. This is where the fire is built with logs and chunks of lava rock which are placed throughout the pile of logs. They're heated in the fire then pulled out and placed in the center of the *Inipi* where water is poured on them.

This is where I am standing, on the outer rim of the fire pit, glancing over the whole scenery, trying to absorb it all. I hear the sound of the drumbeat and the sound of the singers in unison singing traditional songs. The smell of the burnt wood carries through the air, which is cool and still, with the occasional breeze. I watch as the firekeeper (the man in charge of tending the fire) walks around the blazing fire and scorching flames inside the pit. He has a shovel and is moving the logs around so he can start to pull the rocks out of the fire's hot core.

I am a throwaway

I am a throwaway. Labeled by society as
a "menace," discarded and wrote off as a failure,
and an unproductive member of society. Due to
past bad life choices influenced and fueled by
a terminal addiction, I am looked upon as
a cancerous infection upon society's moral
values. I am stripped of rights and opportunities
that limit me like an amputee. However, like
an amputee I have the determination, motivation,
and desire to overcome these limitations. I push,
fight, endure the pain, and continue to be part
of life's race. Despite my limitations, I am a
human being and choose to enjoy life, a life
that is a blessing to me.

I've been fighting this war within myself

I've been fighting this
war within myself
a lifelong battle
ensues
feeling at times
like my sanity
serves as
collateral damage
traumatized
thoughts
night terrors
reclusive tendencies
all after effects
of the conflict within
trust, happiness,
peace, and love
are the unfortunate
and the casualties
of this war

I've been fighting this war within myself

I've been fighting this
war within myself
a lifelong battle
ensues
feeling at times
like my sanity
serves as
collateral damage
traumatized
thoughts
night terrors
reclusive tendencies
all after-effects
of the conflict within
trust, happiness,
peace, and love
are the unfortunates
and the casualties
of this war

solitude

finding stability
in a chemically unbalanced mind
is like searching
for a needle in
a haystack
the constant commotion
the ups
the downs
the highs
the lows
the blitzkrieg of emotions
attacking serenity
amplified anxiety
slight skepticism
bits of paranoia
hinder decision-making
so I find solace
in seclusion
while struggling
with sobriety

only by placing
these fragmented lines
and dissected thoughts
together on paper
does it all come together

Waiting for a call

I am diabetic
I suffer from kidney failure
I also have a malfunctioning pancreas
I was told by doctors
I have about a 2-year wait period
until a donor kidney and pancreas
might be available
Once I am "listed"—meaning
I am placed on a wait list
for a transplant
I am amazed at
modern technology and
modern medicine,
that the transplant procedure
is relatively easy
I am very grateful
that I even have an
opportunity to receive
such a procedure.
However, I feel guilty
about waiting for a call
because in order for
me to receive a kidney
and pancreas
someone has to donate
and being as I don't have
a living donor
someone has to pass away
So for me waiting for a call

means I'm waiting for death,
right?
Someone's death means
I get to live
so is it wrong to wait
on a call?
Either way,
I am granted
another chance
of life,
a true new beginning
so until then
I will be
waiting on a call

Just a thought

I hate being bipolar
            it's awesome

Trainwreck of addiction   By Antonio S.Q.
used to get away
need to escape
So its
full speed ahead
all aboard this
loco-motive
this crazy train
destination unknown
check your baggage
regret, pity, anger, insecurities
theres plenty of room
as your tickets punched
proceed without caution
riding the rails
across the landscape
of insanity
faster than
a speeding bullet
to the brink
flying off the tracks
the bells, the bells, the bells

Train wreck of addiction

Need to get away
need to escape
So it's
full speed ahead
all aboard this
loco-motive
this crazy train
destination unknown
check your baggage
regret, pity, anger, insecurities
there's plenty of room
as your ticket's punched
proceed without caution
riding the rails
across the landscape
of insanity
faster than
a speeding bullet
to the brink
flying off the tracks
the bells, the bells, the bells

I can't fight it (once it's in my blood)

Anger accompanied
by anxiety
woven into the fabric
of insanity of addiction
while splinters
of suffering
embedded in
the soul
itch under
the surface
agitated
aggravated
frustrated it
continues
to be this way
temptation manifested
from trauma
inside the core
of my existence
I can't fight it
this is who I am

Brain chemistry

wicked decisions
landed me in
prison
caged like a
pigeon
in a solitary
position
with a
distorted vision
losin' my religion
reminscin'
of vixens
moral conflictions
cause inner
collisions
my brain chemistry
blames my addictions

Pain 2.0

In my adolescence
I was introduced
to pain
Today, the pain
don't hurt the same
disappointment, betrayal, deceit
been through it all
no one is immune
from life
there are
various degrees
of conflict
there are levels
to this
while a
new hurt
remains on
the horizon
as for today
the pain don't hurt the same

Poem 2.0   Antonio S.D.

In my adolesence
I was introduced
to pain
today, the pain
don't hurt the same
disappointment, betrayal, deciet
been through it all
no one is immune
from life
there are
various degices
of conflict
theres levels
to this
while a
new hurt
remains on
the horizon
as for today,
the pain don't hurt the same

Mead

forever afflicted

Please Mr. Sanchez
start with your
history of
substance abuse

Well, I was first placed
in AA
at the age of nine
By the time
I was 18
I had been back
three fuckin' times
ballistic relapse
damaged my brain
perhaps
smoking back-
to-back blunts
trying to make
my lungs collapse
ate a couple shrooms
visited the dark side
of the moon
seroquel and whiskey
landed me in a padded
room
thoughts distorted
from all the coke
I snorted
messed around

got hooked
and couldn't
afford it
smoked sticks
dipped in water
ate multiple hits
of white blotter
they tried to
get me to quit
in rehab
so I figured
why bother
chemical imbalance
has me addicted
anxiety has me afflicted
if you ask me, doc
I'm forever afflicted

The Hodgepodge (A drunk ain't shit)

Stomach rumbling
it's dinner time
sitting in anticipation
promises of a dinner
consisting of chicken *a la King*
and biscuits.
However, thanks to the cook and
a liter of vodka
the menu had changed
instead I was served
the "Hodgepodge"
which consisted of
a hard-boiled egg
some gummy reheated
mac and cheese
an applesauce cup
and some stale
tortilla chips.
Man, a drunk ain't shit.

Riding a Wave

No stranger
to adversity
the devil is
workin' me
has my mind clouded
with doubt
shadowed with uncertainty
anger-fed addiction
is conducive
so I am
substance abusive
slightly antisocial
so I remain
reclusive
I play the
hand I was dealt
often at war
with self
wish I could
stuff my sorrows
in a sack
and put my worries
on a shelf
untie these
mental knots
just make it
stop
drink after drink

shot after shot
riding a wave
trying to drown out
these intrusive thoughts

fishbowl

Still and vacant
clear and calm
illuminated by
LED lights
awaiting its new
resident

the first occupant
lasted three days
first day seemed fine
new surroundings
happy
On the second day
carefree and happy
on the third day
dead

Occupant number two
again, joyful energetic
on the first day
by dawn of the
next day
floating and cooked
due to a newly-installed
heater
too powerful for
the size of the bowl

So now it sits

awaiting its next victim
an empty fishbowl,
my little death trap

A beautiful disaster

A wave of emotions
crashes down
on the shores
of tranquility
washing away
sands of serenity
under a watchful
moon
reaching out to
the extended hand
to pull me ashore
yet the more I move
the deeper I sink
into the cold
dark abyss

The perfect imperfect

I walk among the twisted shadows
that line the corridors of my mind
seeking retributions for actions
dictated by poison-fed addictions
self-desired isolation hinders
growth deemed necessary for
victory against this lifelong adversary
the continuous fight wears me
   down
each battle in this war ends
with greater casualties and
increasing collateral damage
and an ever-growing void
within
even when things on the outside
appear under control
on the inside, chaos
reigns supreme
to scratch the surface
is to open pandora's box
and unleash what lies within
pain, betrayal, vengeance
self-sabotaging saints
in the cathedral—
that is me

Doppelganger

You,
You and your arrogant attitude
                you're better than no one

You size yourself up, thinking you can't be touched
                you bleed just like everyone else

You think you're so smart with your level of education
                you're idiotic for the things you do

You think you are in control
                you don't control anything,
                  including your life

You think you're calm, cool and collected
                it's an image, you're a powder keg
                waitin' to blow

You call yourself honest and real
                yet you lie, cheat and steal

You with your "holier than thou" talk
                you're far from a goddamn Saint

You call yourself a father
                you're a stranger to your own
                children

You think you beat your addiction
                            it's a lifelong battle

You think your girl can't live without you
                            you've already been replaced

You try to get the lightest sentence for your crime
                          be a man and face the consequences, if
                             you get what you truly deserve you
                           would be serving a life sentence

When I look into your eyes, what I hate most
                Is that you're me

Consumed

Consumed by my vices
chewed up and spat out
by my addictions
regurgitated from within
the belly of the beast
what's leftover
is now a phantom existence
lost in my own personal
wrinkle in time
a memory to some
a reminder of others past
a stranger to my children
but still I live
and through these words
my voice is heard

Trip

Paranoia, schizophrenia, psychosis
due to multiple LSD doses

voices in my head
have me seeing red
fuck the world
and all that's on it
rage burns like
the heat of a comet

everyone lies
for self gain
no one is immune
from goin' insane

jaws clench as
back starts to
ache
anticipation of
visions that await

two-person personality
two views of reality
one hell of a trip

The King

Damnation of my mind
curses on my soul
the warmth of my
heart turned
bitter cold

rejection of love
denial of truth
comfort of being
a social recluse
branded by distrust
scared by hate
bear witness
to that which
manipulation helped create

ruined forever
and forever alone
in the kingdom of
eternal solitude
I sit on my throne

Lothario

The first sip
is always bitter
reluctance to unleash the other
personalities within
the demon
the jokester
the badass
the emotional wretch
uncertainty of which will
emerge as comprehension and
reality fade to black
only to emerge from an
alcohol induced abyss
hopefully unscathed and
with all senses intact
damage control is now in order
and soft shame and disappointment
oversee all
as the thirst remains unquenched
dry heaving, purging the bile
of a past, present and unseen future
gut-wrenching spasms
that leave the body aching
and the promise to never
consume the poison again
realizing that the only antidote
is the very poison that induced
these very feelings
    the hair of the dog

All aboard this crazy train

All aboard this crazy train
next stop: chaos
the loco-motive
runs on rage, alcohol and drugs
hold onto your ticket
'cause it's full speed ahead
everyone has luggage and
it's standin' room only
I'm your (con)doctor
you hear the whistle blow
that means it's time to go
let's roll!

Relapse

The cravings manifest
out of boredom
creep into my
subconscious
infecting my thoughts
clouding my judgement:

just one more time
to take the pain away
no one has to know
this is the last time

the three greatest lies
told

Sprung

Let me lick
your tears
and taste
the salt
of your lies
feed my narcissistic desires
because that's how I like it.
You know the game, baby—
hurt me, make it deep
to the core,
you'll be my new-found addiction
as I fiend for more.

Antonio

Scooter

Scooter scuffled around
in his jailhouse sandals
orange jumpsuit unbuttoned
and fastened around
his waist
his dingy white t-shirt
with a stretched out collar
hung loosely on his old
withered frame
anxiously organizing
his cards
Spades was his game
and he was spade tight
hoping his partner
would follow suit
no poker face here
Scooter smiled a big
toothless grin
four man pics
are on the line
he plays

Invict

I've a
I have
I've
I, fi
  bea
  bea
  a
  m
  s,

The Rebuild

I am at a point in my life where t
or life should I say, are coming full c
I call the past years of my life 1990-
the teardown. In that time I endured
knives, fists, boots, and bottles. All the
drinking while having a chronic illness t
deteriorated my kidneys.
Now, I am living a new lifestyle. On
healing. This part of my life I call t
I have put my demons to rest. Made ~~wra~~
with myself and to most I have
the past. I help instead of hurt, a

III - Incarceration:

this concrete coffin

Sweat Lodge (Part III)

As I stand there, I stare at the fire. I see how its flames seem to be doing a dance, swaying, weaving and reaching up to the sky. Its muffled rumble interrupted by snaps and pops as it consumes the logs that rest in its belly. It draws energy from the wood and uses that energy to grow in size and heat. Its orange and reddish hue pulsating as if it is taking preparatory deep breaths before it releases its true power. Like it is purposely trying to intimidate me. Taunting me, telling me I won't be able to withstand its heat and to not even try. Occasionally reaching out and stinging my face as the wind causes its heat to shift and move in my direction and giving a brief preview of what's to come. Being mesmerized by the fire's enchanting dance my trance-like mind state is suddenly broke.

"Let's go, *Tushka*," (*Tushka* meaning warrior) says a bold Southern voice next to me. The voice belonging to Rob Collins, my closest friend since coming to prison and my mentor in learning these Native American practices and ways. Rob is a 30-year-old full-blooded Choctaw from Southern Oklahoma. He stands at about 5' 10" with an athletic frame, long black hair flowing like silk, stopping at about the middle of his back. His facial features are plain and common of the typical

Native American. A face that looks like its structure is stone, expressionless with no facial hair, high cheek bones, a handsome jaw line, and a bridged nose that two dark brown eyes rest atop of.

"Remember, nothing in that lodge can or is meant to hurt you," he says. "Don't focus on the pain, the physical, when the steam gets hot, focus on the prayers and the songs being sung. It makes your medicine that much stronger. If you gotta get out, it's okay, it's not a macho thing. But if you can, try to stay in. If it gets too hot, lay down. Remember, *focus,* you'll do just fine, let's go." As he said, "let's go," his hand gave my shoulder a heavy-handed pat and a firm squeeze.

The guys have prepared the lodge, it has been covered with a layer of blankets, followed by a worn green military tarp, then topped off with more blankets to keep the sunlight out and to trap the heat inside the lodge.

The sweat lodge leaders (the guys who run the ceremony) have already entered the lodge and blessed it, burning sage and cedar, saying prayers and also burning sweetgrass to evoke all bad spirits and invoke good ones. The doorway to the lodge looks like an opening to a dark cave, and I anticipate what lies within.

I take my place in line amongst the other guys going in. Everyone is stripped down to their boxers. Some carry hand towels, some wear bandanas of different colors and patterns in various styles on their heads. Each man doing their own little personal ritual before they enter the lodge. Some pour water on themselves from a dipper in a plastic bucket sitting on the ground. Others grab handfuls of sage and cedar and rub it on their bodies to purify themselves. Some just stand still, no movement, eyes closed in a moment of brief prayer. The remaining men stand holding their arms wrapped around their waists as if trying to warm themselves from the brisk morning chill. As each man enters, he gets down on all fours and bows down, head touching the ground, and says "*mitakye oasin*," Lakota words honoring the Creator. Each man then crawls into the lodge on his hands and knees. I stand in line and feel the adrenaline rush, a surge of energy shoots through my mind and my body. Mentally I feel ready as ever. I just hope the physical is prepared. The man before me (Rob) just went in, now it's my turn.

I step to the entrance of the doorway. I give one last look up to the sky. The morning sun has fully emerged and is illuminating the entire sky with hardly any clouds. I close my eyes, take a deep breath and lower myself on all fours. I bow my head to the earth and say my prayer for strength, wisdom and forgiveness. I proceed to crawl into the lodge.

The Watcher

I arrived at Saline County Jail in Salina, Kansas, after being transferred from KDOC (Kansas Department of Corrections), to settle an unresolved sentencing on a burglary charge. I had been serving time already in KDOC for a prior case and was resolving matters of the pending charges.

Since my arrival, I was a troublesome indivi-dual—not in the sense of immature or rambunctious behavior. Troublesome in the sense of my defiant attitude towards the facility's rules, and what I viewed as power-hungry guards with control issues. Having already had a taste of what prison life was like, County Jail rules seemed petty and minimal to me. I had several conflicts of interest with many of the guards. After several rule violations, infractions and a final confron-tation with a guard, I ended up where all rule violators go: Segregation, otherwise known as "the hole."

Saline County Jail's segregation unit was of standard format of that day and age. The unit was a separate pod from the rest of General Population where all the other inmates were housed. The pod consisted of twelve individual cells, six on ground level, six on an upper tier, accessible by a metal staircase. The dayroom area was comprised of a couple metal tables with connecting stools, a shower stall with plastic curtain, and a big window for observation by the officers seated at the control desk on the other side of the glass.

As I was escorted to my cell in handcuffs, I was restrained by an officer on each side of me, gripping onto my arms. Upon my arrival into the pod, the only sound in the unit was my voice as I yelled obscenities at the guards. As I shouted my disdain for the guards and the facility's rules, my voice carried loud and the echoes reverberated back in a resounding amplified tone.

In the dimly lit pod, as I slowly approached my cell, I noticed the opened metal door to my designated chamber and how it looked like a mouth to a dark hungry cave waiting to consume me. The guards fed me to the hole, and the huge metal door swallowed me as it roared and was sealed shut with a thunderous slam. The next thing I heard was the jingling of the officer's keys and the unlocking of the beanhole in the center of the door. The beanhole slammed as it fell open and the officer said, "Back up." I moved back until my back was flush against the door and placed my hands in the opening of the beanhole and the officer proceeded to unlock the handcuffs, freeing my hands. As soon as the handcuffs were off, the beanhole was slammed shut. I yelled, "How long am I here for?" No reply, the only response was the fading footsteps of the officer's boots as they exited the pod, followed by the boom of the main door to the pod as they left.

Standing there in my newly appointed cell, I rubbed my wrists, loosening the tension from the tight grasp of the metal restraints. I looked around at the cell. It consisted of four cinder-block walls painted white, a white concrete slab ceiling with two fluorescent bulbs encased in a metal trapezoidal cover in the center. The cell was furnished with a concrete slab built two cinder blocks high, wall to wall in length. The slab was topped with a plastic mattress, which was to serve as my bed. The cell also had a small metal table painted gray and bolted to the wall by two parallel brackets on its under-side. The table was placed at bedside so I could use the slab as a seat so I could sit and eat my meals. There was also a metal toilet and sink combination unit with built-in cylindrical space for a small toilet roll. Right above the sink was a small square polished metal mirror fastened to the wall by screws along its outer frame.

Glancing around my cell I took notice of the rectangular window on the far wall above the table. It was night-time so the window appeared as a framed picture of black. These were the contents of my confinement quarters.

I faced the metal door, looked through the glass and yelled, "Hey!" My voice bounced off the walls and I was answered by the echo of my own voice. I yelled a couple more times. The only reply was the repetition of my voice. It was then that I realized . . . I was alone.

After my discovery of my isolation in "the hole," I lay on the mattress and stared at the light fixture and cursed my situation. I lay there and pondered about how long I would be in solitary confinement. It was not my first time in solitary, I had been in various county jails including my multiple trips to the jail in my hometown, Lawrence. In my personal opinion, if you've seen one jail then you've seen them all. I was not troubled by my time in the hole, because I didn't know anyone in general population and they were squares and weirdos in my eyes. Small town people in a small town jail, "Fuck 'em," I thought. I lay there, closed my eyes and faded off into a surprisingly deep sleep.

I awoke to the sound of a guard fumbling with his keys to open the beanhole, which meant it was breakfast time. The beanhole slammed open and a plastic tray was placed in the open slot. The guard said, "Breakfast," and I said, "Nope." I was still lying down and I had barely opened my eyes. I squinted as the morning light burned my eyes. I heard the guard remove the tray and close the beanhole. Then the sound of the guard exiting the pod.

I shielded my eyes with my forearm and resumed my slumber.

Time and time again

Time and time again/I end up back in the
pen/sittin' in a cell trapped in my sin/tryin' to
rewind/memories in my mind/to a better place and
time/as I sit in tha land where the blind
lead the blind

my incarceration is how I atone/for
mi vida loca in the zone/yet I refuse
to call this place home

years in this cage is how I atone/for
mi vida loca in tha zone/with my hand on the
chrome/invadin' people's homes/now I'm in tha
belly of tha beast/worse off than bein' on
them streets

It's getting old

It's getting old
repeating myself
making same choices
the same consequences
the same circumstances
from taking penitentiary chances
to make financial advances

it's getting old
looking at life thru a beanhole

it's getting old
sittin' waitin' on a ghost letter
they said they mailed it but I know better

it's getting old
the only visit is by an attorney
sittin' in front of a jury

it's getting' old
seein' the pain in my mama's eyes
doin' wrong no matter how hard I try

Self-imprisoned (my only fear)   By Antonio S.Q.

Locked in a cage
at the age of 18
eventually consumed by rage
over a quarter of
a century later
and no out date
he let the anger within
dictate his fate
family and friends
evaporated through time
bonds created
broke
then ~~fully~~ left behind
pushed to the brink
he made a final decision
for an eternal stay
and to be
forever self-imprisoned

Self-imprisoned (my only fear)

Locked in a cage
at the age of 18
eventually consumed by rage
over a quarter of
a century later
and no out date
he let the anger within
dictate his fate
family and friends
evaporated through time
bonds created
broke
then left behind
pushed to the brink
he made a final decision
for an eternal stay
and to be
forever self-imprisoned

The place I go

isolated with
this pain
accompanied by regret
in this cold world
anger keeps me warm
like a shot of whiskey
revenge gives me
purpose
vengeance motivates
this is the place
I go
before I do wrong

The day's last cigarette

He had been smoking
since he was 16 years old
now at age 45,
a seasoned convict
four years in on a
seventeen-year bid
smoking the day's
last cigarette
D.O.C. had made
cigarettes illegal contraband
effective tomorrow
the prison commissary
stopped selling tobacco products
last week
so cigarettes were already
damn near obsolete
inmates all over the prison compound
had secret tobacco stash spots
myself included
I had purchased as many pouches
of tobacco as I could
the previous week at commissary
and had already had most
of them packed and buried
last cigarette
in a PVC tube
out on the yard
the remaining few
I kept for last

minute sales to
the highest bidder
and here he was
standing in front of me
huffin' and puffin'
Twenty-five dollars
for a three-dollar pouch
of tobacco
and a half an hour
to smoke it before
the ban went into effect
I didn't think he could
do it, and had nothing
but time, so I watched him
roll one, smoke one,
cough, hack, spit
repeat
I watched in amazement
as he smoked
one after another
face leathery and gray
last cigarette
he inhaled and exhaled
smoking like a broke
down muffler
as time winded down.
If emphysema had a face
it was his—
my lungs hurt watching
this display of desperation
as he truly smoked
the day's last cigarette

Jailhouse coffee

An arm's length of string
from a pair of socks
wrapped around a pencil
placed into an empty envelope
creates the Cadillac as we call it
I get on my hands and knees
look under the tiny space
under my heavy metal cell door
see my target
the daylit space under
my neighbor's cell door
"ready" I yell
"ready" my neighbor replies
I slide the envelope with
full force
the Cadillac arrives effortlessly
anxious I hop up and look
to see if any guards noticed
none

I get back onto the
cold concrete floor
I see shadows move
in the space under my
neighbor's door
"ok go" my neighbor yells
"pull!"
I pull excitedly with
a hand-over-fist motion

the sound of weighted paper
sliding on concrete
announces the arrival
of the envelope under my door
I grab the envelope with
my fingertips
clutch the envelope
and take a whiff,
ah, yes!
I tear the end of
the envelope open
dump the contents
in my cup and
rush to the sink
press the hot water button
repeatedly
flush the toilet simultaneously
check the water temp
when its lukewarm
I place the cup under

taking a sip
I exhale with
a sigh of relief
now all I need
is a cigarette

Wordplay

Count time
lockdown
chow
yard
lockdown
every day is Groundhog Day
the epitome of repetition
and I wonder why
institutionalization
is an issue
pat downs, strip searches
and cell inspections
are the norm here
seeing someone get their
head split open like a
cantaloupe is a typical day
eating lunch while someone
is rushed off to the hospital
is proper etiquette here

where did the angels go
'cause all I see is demons
lord, I pray for the return
of happy times

Scooter

Antonio

Scooter scuffled around
in his jailhouse sandals
orange jumpsuit unbuttoned
and fastened around
his waist
his dingy white t-shirt
with a streched out collar
hung losely on his old
withered frame
anxiously organizing
his cards
Spades was his game
and he was spade tight
hoping his partner
would follow suit
no poker face here
Scooter smiled a big
toothles grin
four monpies
are on the line
and he plays
to win

Scooter

Scooter scuffled around
in his jailhouse sandals
orange jumpsuit unbuttoned
and fastened around
his waist
his dingy white t-shirt
with a stretched-out collar
hung loosely on his old
withered frame
anxiously organizing
his cards
Spades was his game
and he was spade tight
hoping his partner
would follow suit
no poker face here
Scooter smiled a big
toothless grin
four Moon Pies
are on the line
and he plays
to win

Catch 22

Incarcerated
stuck in a sandbox
as the quicksands
of time
pour against me
looking out of
a beanhole
with a panoramic
view of the world
watching life
pass me by
as life proceeds
without me
and those closest
to me either
fade away or move on
them same people
after my release
stay stuck
in the past

I did my time
for my crimes
But I get treated
like my crime
was doing time

Winner, Winner

I've seen this before, anticipation. People arriving
early, taking their place in line. Excitement brewing,
people buzzing. Waiting for the hot new thing. If
supplies run out, mass hysteria. When the spicy
chicken sandwich hit in Norton Correctional Facility,
inmates lost their minds. Trying to double back in line,
dropping their trays on the floor, placing hair on their
pieces of chicken, any shenanigans to get another
spicy chicken patty. It was not uncommon
for CO's to find chicken stash spots. In the
chow hall, under tables. On the yard, under the bleachers,
even in the library, in the encyclopedia, pages stained
by greasy goodness. I even once had to take a loss
of four patties I stocked in a bush to a territorial,
greedy opossum.

The other day I seen on the news, a reminder
of the days in Norton. I witnessed the familiar
lines, the mass hysteria, even fights, over a chicken
sandwich at Popeyes across the nation. There's
something about a chicken sandwich . . .

Blindspot

I remember sitting in my cell, laying on my back one night. Just another day in the pen coming to an end with me watching a San Antonio Spurs basketball game, until I drifted off into a deep sleep.

I woke up the next morning and went to med line. Up before sunrise and with a stocking cap pulled low, I didn't notice anything different about my vision. Other than a slight blur, all seemed normal. Walking across the compound, I took notice of a haze in my vision. So I rubbed my eyes and carried on. Stepping into the cell house, the bright fluorescent bulbs that burned endlessly intensified the haze. As soon as I returned to my cell I washed my face again, thinking I may have caught something in my eye, but I didn't feel any itch, scratch or irritation.

I had eyedrops, placed a couple of drops in each eye, yet nothing changed. Things seemed out of focus. When I turned on my TV, all I could see was a blur. It wasn't until my cellie got up and I tried to explain what was going on that I noticed something alarming. A faceless image stood before me. I started to panic: *I couldn't see.* After calling on my intercom down to the control booth, explaining my situation, I was allowed to go to the infirmary.

That walk was probably one of the scariest walks I've taken, ever, walking across the yard in a Maximum Security prison, blind. Living the life of a gang member, I had plenty of enemies, people who would not hesitate to attack me, if they had the chance. Enemies that I was currently at war with, and on S.O.S. status: *Smash On Sight*. See an enemy, attack them. Yet here I was, not able to see anything. All I could see was shapes and colors. Walking alone, fearful, in one big blindspot. Every inmate I passed, I couldn't differentiate, friend or foe. Anxious and apprehensive with each shape that approached, skittish as I turned every corner, ready for an assault at any time.

I made it to the infirmary, squinting all the way, behind my commissary-issued sunglasses.

After being seen by the nurses and finally the doctor, I was diagnosed as legally blind. My diabetes had affected my vision, and my blood pressure was so high it caused pressure on the back of my eyes, against my eyeballs, distorting my vision.

Blind, in prison, only able to see shapes and colors.

Shit, how long was this to last? Is it permanent? How was I going to live my life? How would I function? Why, God, why?

At that moment, I felt something I hadn't felt in a long time. A hot wetness rolled down my cheeks, tears.

Tears at the thought of losing my sight. How was I going to function? How was I going to survive what remaining time I had in prison?

How was I going to write if I could not see the words on paper?

Lord show me the way

I blow trees with no discretion
askin' Jehovah for direction
and give my obsession with this drug profession
and of evil deeds
driven by lust and greed
as I proceed to make my block bleed
Now is there a heaven
for this barrio legend
a five-time felon
committin' 2-11's
and these weed-laced observations
is givin' me patience
thru all these fucked-up situations
I've been facin' since creation
searchin' for salvation
from repeated incarceration
smokin' my last blunt with no moderation
pursuin' false illusions
endless mass confusion
with the only intrusion
from this weed I'm abusin'
nocturnal premonitions
full of admonitions
are givin' me vision
buildin' my ambition
to proceed on my mission

Blank

Shattered remains of a life once lived
reached my boiling point, nothing more to give
all hope is lost, all faith depleted
feeling like my life's journey is now completed
belief that nothing exists beyond death
just awaiting that final breath
failed at all throughout this pitiful life
so many unsuccessful opportunities to get it right
abandoned by my father, abhorred by my mother
then my sister in law, isolated from my brother
separated from my precious son and beloved daughter
mislead by friends, like sheep to a slaughter
life is what you make it . . . I've made mine hell
so in this concrete coffin I shall dwell

Possibilities

Sitting here pondering
my current situation
my mind runs rampant
with possibilities of my outcome:

I could get probation
I could get a chance of rehab
I could get back on those streets
I could get back with my girl
I could find a wealthy woman
I could hang with the old crew
I could drink one beer and smoke
    just one joint
I could jump back in the game
I could hit one final big lick
I could do one big final deal
I could win it all
    be happy and rich
    and get out the game
    without getting caught

Sorry, y'all, I'm out of dreams for sale

It's Crazy

It's crazy to think 37 ounces of steel
used to hold me down
15 on the wrists
22 on the ankles
    man, it's crazy

Dark clouds of my mind

In the dark clouds of my mind
an eternal vail of twilight
canopies a dominion of darkness
light is eclipsed permanently
in this desolate realm

However I am not alone
on the devil's darkside
for I sit in the company of
murderers, blasphemers, adulterers and thieves
in this legion of demons
the archangel Michael reigns supreme

here the scent of sulfur
scorches my nostrils
screams of agony and torment
pierce my ears
my teeth grind to powder
and my tears evaporate
as my spirit is whipped 39 times
with a cat of 9 tails

repeated crucifixion of my soul
because I am something
less than God
and my conviction is just

Not a movie

Ten o'clock, it's showtime. Every night
I get my own personal, private viewing.
I lay back in my concrete theatre as the
lights go out and the projector protrudes
from my forehead and starts running the film.

The following feature is rated "R" (real), for
graphic images of anger, frustration, hate,
stubbornness, rage, jealousy, anguish, hurt,
humiliation, shame, and immense pain.

This is a work of non-fiction, names,
characters, places, and incidents are not
products of the author's imagination, they are
used non-fictitiously, and are not to be
construed as fiction. All resemblance to actual
events, places, organizations, and people
living and dead is entirely real. This is
not a movie, this is my life . . .

The Brown Recluse

Alone, silently I sit
in the farthest corner
of every room I inhabit
isolated solitarily in my web
with the sight of hundreds
of eyes
watching all that passes
studying all movement
observing every action
prepared to strike
to protect what's mine

the hairs on my arms and legs
tingle at the slightest threat
secluded in my solitude
anxiously awaiting
my prey is void of innocence
their dishonesty and betrayal
lead them to my elaborately
spun web

my venom is their atonement
which decomposes
their merciless being
vengeance is not
my intent
it is retribution
for my own sin

The engine of incarceration

The engine of incarceration
is primed with aggression, pain
and loneliness
with a turn of the master key
this motor of mundanity
which is housed in steel and wire
roars to life

The pistons of this prison
fire up
with a rumble of the cell doors
as they roll open
followed by the thunderous—SLAM!
as they close

vociferous tales of lives once lived
amplified by beats
created by closed fists pounding
on tables, walls and chests
verbose conversations aided by
forced belches and farts
reverberate off the steel walls

only to be interrupted
by the booming voice on the P.A. system
directing inmate movement to programs and yard
a steady stream of water splashes
on the concrete floor of the showers
in the distance

with repetitive interjections of WHOOSH!
as a toilet flushes

bird whistles echo
signaling the presence
of a guard in the cellhouse
constant squawking and alarms blaring
on the walkie-talkies of those very
guards signaling fights and medical emergencies
throughout the facility
the jingle of a guard's keys as he walks
confirm his whereabouts
playing cards slapping
the metal surface of tables
accompanied by the explosive—BANG!
of heavy ivory dominoes striking similar surfaces
throughout the cell block
Stereos blasting all kinds of music
each one drowning out the next
in a constant battle for dominant volume

As the engine is shut off
and cools for the night
an eerie silence develops
and gives birth to
the most clamorous and unstoppable
sound of this machine

which is the voices in my head

That Man

I am often awakened at the same time (2:30 a.m.)
by an obscure presence
a shadow overlooking my bedside
from the corner of my cell

within the somberness that envelopes
my concrete chamber
this particular silhouette
overshadows the rest of the
configurations that encompass
my dismal surroundings

an artic shiver trembles through
my body as I acknowledge
the apparent nightly presence
of this apparition
which resembles the form of
a person, which is why I call it "that man"

there are no distinguishing details or features
that define its gender or
its overall demeanor
there's no movement, it just
awaits . . . motionless

it does not make a sound
its overbearing silence amplifies
its enigmatic poise and intensifies
my fear

yet this nightly visitor doesn't
harm me
who or what is it?
A demon, a guardian?
Something to protect me or
a night traveler to harm me

Slam

The slam of cold steel
rattles the brain
while sending shivers
down the spine
thunderous repeated slams
pierce the eardrum
and echo in the corridors
of the mind
continuous from
various distances
syncopation of the senses
tapping on the nerves
eroding sanity
such a sinister lullaby

Getting out

Lost in my own
wrinkle in time
while the world kept
turning
friends now raising families
family members grown older
children are now no longer
adolescents
   new city streets
sides of town expanded
technological advances
culture shock
trying to adjust
is like jumping in a
raging river
trying not to get swept
away in the current

Dark Confusion

In the deepest darkest
corridors of my mind
dwell my demons
creatures with chains
that bind
tyrants that torment
twist my thoughts
and distort my perception

caretakers of carnal desires
masters of mental manipulation
embed splinters of insanity
deep in my mind

consistent attempts to tame these beasts
create ever-present conflict and confusion
while parasitic emotions decay my soul

lunacy runs rampant
in this labyrinth of lividity
futile attempts at prayer
to a God that failed

Vato loco Boy

Tired of chasing vices
  and material devices
worn and weathered
skin tougher than leather
'cause pain don't hurt
help create
what I became
vato loco Boy
turned penitentiary
poet

planted a seed
of change
and watered it
with knowledge
to grow it
a voice for
those who
endure the struggle

Inside Locked Doors

Secured seclusion
Motivation obsolete
Appetite diminished
Motion stagnant
Life wilting away
As the sands of time
Fall
Anhedonia
Consumed and digested by
The beast that is
Depression
Suffering while possessing
A self-conviction
This is the best way
Inside locked doors,
While those on the
Outside looking in
Suffer right along
Beside you

Alone in my cell

Alone in my cell
often I felt
defeated before
I started
me against the world
segregated from everything
I ever cared about
isolated
then I began to realize
the more I lost
the more I gained
friends, money, street fame
all a façade

Antonio S.O.

Invictus

I've danced in the shadows of the moon
I have flown too close to the sun
I've ran with the devil
I flirted with death for fun
been grazed by a bullet
been sliced by a blade
all while enduring a chronic illness
most of my days
Spent my life makin my bones
now I just wanna rest them
by the fire
Call me "invictus", unconquered
when I retire

I've

I've
war
a lif
ensu
feel
like
se
c

Scooter

Scooter scuffled around
in his jailhouse sandals
orange jumpsuit unbuttoned
and fastened around
his waist
his dingy white t-shirt
with a streched out collar
hung losely on his old
withered frame
anxiously organizing

IV. Transformation

a second chance of life

I've been fighting this war within myself

I've been fighting this
war within myself
a lifelong battle
ensues
feeling at times
like my sanity
serves as
collateral damage
traumatized
thoughts
night terrors
reclusive tendencies
all after effects
of the conflict within
trust, happiness,
peace, and love
are the unfortunates
and the casualties

I write because
I write because...

I am somewhat introv
with a dose of alexit

write because...

unclutters my mind
es the negativity
replenishes peace
holding my demons

e because....

-discovery
tal freedom

because ...
testimony
er of writ

Antonio

A mile in my shoes   By Antonio

I had once seen an interview with Mr. T, where he
made a valid point and influenced me. In his interview
he wore his usual attire, sweat pants, a muscle tee, and
of course was adorned with several gold chains, to accen
his trademark mohawk.

During the interview the reporter poked fun at his
shoes, some ragged sneakers. Mr. T's response to
the reporters comments was: "I wear them, because they
remind me of where I came from, before I got famous

Sweat Lodge (Part IV)

I follow Rob in a clockwise motion crawling around the pit that looks like a mouth opening from the Earth's crust. The ground's cold to my hands and fingers, the ground is hard and covered with cedar that's been sprinkled on the ground. I find my place next to Rob on the Northern direction of the lodge, following the order in which we entered. I sit up with my back straight and my legs crossed, with my arms resting on my legs. I watch as the remaining men enter.

The smell of the cedar, sage, and sweetgrass that has been burnt inside the lodge is heavy, and there's a light cloud of smoke lingering in the air. I look around the lodge and see the faces of these men I am about to suffer with. Everyone is seated in the same fashion and all are silent, just sitting there, each man preparing his mind and body for the rocks that are about to be brought in.

The last man enters and is seated.

On the left hand side of the doorway sits the sweat lodge leader, the man who will run the ceremony. His name is Kumali, he is part Hawaiian, part Apache. He's in his mid-40s, has all the distinguishing facial features of Native Americans, his hair is long and coarse and he has the physique of a man who has done physical labor all his life. Big barrel chest, broad shoulders and muscular arms. He is somewhat hunched over the pit as he sprinkles sage into the pit as he silently prays.

Next to him is his helper. This man's responsibility is to assist the sweat leader in singing and arranging the rocks as they're placed in the pit. His name is Dion, a big man from the Dakota Hidatsu Nation. He sits in the formal position, but his huge frame gives the impression that whichever way he sits, he's going to be uncomfortable because of his size. Yet he sits peacefully and quietly. In his right hand is a fan made of hawk feathers. Its four feathers are about the same size and length as butcher's knives; they overlap each other and are united at the base by a piece of tan buckskin wrapped and sewn around the quills. The fan is used to move the steam around in the lodge after the water is poured on the rocks. Resting in Dion's lap is a small flat drum. It's in the shape of a stop sign and has a wooden frame with a buffalo hide dried and stretched to wrap around the frame and is sewn on its outer edges by leather strands. The drum is played as songs are sung during the ritual, and it is also his responsibility to lead the songs.

Kumali speaks to us about what we are all gathered in the lodge for and reminds us to stay strong. He tells us that we have come to give of ourselves, to sacrifice our pain, to strengthen our prayers. That we have come to clear our mind, body and spirit of the stress, confusion, anger, worries and all the negative energy that we get overburdened with in our daily existence. He explains how the lodge resembles our mother's womb when we were inside. How it was dark, hot, uncomfortable, how that's what it's about to be like. But how when we step out the lodge, we will be reborn, cleansed of all that negativity.

"Hot Rocks" is yelled by the firekeeper outside the entrance to the lodge. I see his legs standing at the outer left side of the entrance. A wooden handled digging shovel slides in the lodge. A pile of about six medium-sized lava rocks rest in the shovel. The shovel is slid to the lip of the pit and Dion leans over the pit and uses a deer antler to scoop the rocks off the shovel and into the pit. I hear the thud of the rocks as they land in the pit. I can instantly feel the dry heat off the rocks.

Kumali reaches out his arm and sprinkles sage and cedar on the rocks to purify them. Soon as the sage and cedar land on the rocks, they burst into tiny flames forming streams of smoke, and the cedar makes a popping sound as it burns from the heat of the rocks. The little flames doing the same dance as the big flames of the larger fire outside. Swaying, poking up towards the sky, teasing, taunting me again. I feel the dry heat and imagine what it will be like when all rocks are placed in the fire pit and the water poured on them. Three more loads of rocks are brought in, and with each load that's placed in the pit in front of me, I feel the heat gradually grow. A bucket of water is brought in. I am trying to absorb everything using all my senses, then I close my eyes.

"Is everyone ready to begin?" Kumali asks. All the men in the lodge nod, signaling their readiness.

"Allright then, door!" says Kumali.

Any work will do

$9.50
operating an
industrial mixer
a monster of a machine
for ten-hour shifts
seven days a week
mixing
tons of macaroni salad
and potato salad
daily
getting sprayed with
water, mustard, mayonnaise
and relish
in a constant
thirty-two degree
cooker
pushing, pulling
five-hundred-pound metal
cannisters consistently
twilight clock-ins
evening clock-outs
one-hour bus rides
to and from
no issues with
my criminal history
or lack of a college
degree
starting over
on parole
I will take it
'cause any work will do

livin' in the last days of revelation

it's time for a spiritual elevation as a nation
we're all beautiful minds and wondrous creations
individual links in a universal hoop
survivin' on hell's front porch; tha devil's stoop

wishin' I could change the world, but I can only
    change myself
prayin', searchin', seekin', pleadin' for help
plagued with addiction, infected with hate
this mental prison I can't escape

playin' devil's advocate; satan's servant
a ship lost at sea, swept away in the current
creator for my anchor, please hold me down
keep my head above water and don't let me drown

let me face my demons, one and all
stand and deliver, no longer withdrawal
then give me wings and let me fly
help me leave this life of sin behind

One day I'll get it together

One day I'll get it together/better later than never

nobody wants to hire a Mex-ex con/guess I'm payin'
the price for all tha shit I've done/cast out of society,
voted off the island/family stabbin' me in the back
while they fake smilin'

nothin' out here pans out like I thought
I'm a big fish in a small pond
out there I'm plankton in a sea
all I know is the prison life, struggle
and strife, ain't no retirement for an
ex-con, it's hard days till I'm
in tha dirt

Tryin' to make a change
one day I'll get it together/make a change
for tha better/

I write because (word play)

I write because
it's sunny outside
so I must describe
and paint a picture
with my words
of the beauty
of the day

I write because
its getting old
harboring these negative
thoughts

I write because
who I am right now
is a changed man that
stands before you
and my story
is a conduit
of change

I write because
writing keeps me
anchored
through stormy weather

I write because
through healing
and self-love

there are
good things
to come
like a second
chance of life
in more ways
than one

A mile in my shoes

I had once seen an interview with Mr. T., where he
made a valid point and influenced me. In his interview,
he wore his usual attire—sweat pants, a muscle tee, and
of course he was adorned with several gold chains, to accent
his trademark mohawk.

During the interview, the reporter poked fun at his
shoes, some ragged sneakers. Mr. T's response to
the reporter's comments was: "I wear them because they
remind me of where I come from, before I got rich and
famous."

I chose to apply that to my own life, with my own
sneakers. See these fat-tongued Vans on my feet are
the shoes I wore in prison. These shoes have walked plenty
of miles. My friends have had a good laugh at my
foot attire. I get teased 'cause I wear these shoes still.

I wear them as a reminder, a reminder of where I came
from behind them walls. Also, as a reminder that
every step I take is one step away from going back.
Yes, I've changed, however I'm still in the same shoes.
I have several other pairs of shoes, but these have
meaning, and honestly they're comfortable. Those who
have walked a mile in my shoes know what I mean.

A mile in my shoes   By Antonio SO

    I had once seen an interview with Mr. T, where he
made a valid point and influenced me. In his interview
he wore his usual attire, sweat pants, a muscle tee, and
of course was adorned with several gold chains, to accent
his trademark mohawk.

    During the interview the reporter poked fun at his
shoes, some ragged sneakers. Mr. T's response to
the reporters comments was, "I wear them, because they
remind me of where I came from, before I got famous
and money."

    I chose to apply that to my own life, with my own
sneakers. See these fat tongued, Vans on my feet are
the shoes I wore in Prison. These shoes have walked plenty
of miles. My friends have had a good laugh at my
foot attire. I get teased cause I wear these shoes still.
I wear them as a reminder, a reminder of where I came
from behind them walls. Also as a reminder that
every step I take is one step away from going back.
Yes, I've changed, however I still am in the same shoes.
I have several other pairs of shoes, but these have
meaning, and honestly they're comfortable. For those
who have walked a mile in my shoes, know what
mean.

Invictus   Antonio S.O.

I've danced in the shadows of the moon
I have flown too close to the sun
I've ran with the devil
I flirted with death for fun
been grazed by a bullet
been sliced by a blade
all while enduring a chronic illness
most of my days
Spent my life makin my bones
now I just wanna rest them
by the fire
Call me "invictus"; unconquered
when I retire

Invictus

I've danced in the shadows of the moon
I have flown too close to the sun
I've ran with the devil
I flirted with death for fun

been grazed by a bullet
been sliced by a blade
all while enduring a chronic illness
most of my days

spent my life makin' my bones
now I just wanna rest them
by the fire
call me "Invictus;" unconquered
when I retire

My motivation

I refuse to believe
all of us are the
unfortunates, the worthless,
the dregs of society.
No, we are at an advantage—
we have been in places and
in positions
others haven't.

Being in those places and positions
made us tap into an inner strength
others never get to discover.
It has been said:
"Only through pain do we achieve greatness."
Our skills are sharpened,
we have achieved a heightened sense
of awareness
and we are in a position
to turn it around.

We are the broken and afflicted—
this is my motivation

Pains and Perils

I've danced
in the shadows
of the moon
I have flown
too close
to the sun
Spent years chasing
the ghost
in the web
of addiction I spun

graveyard in my closet
exhumed memories
resuscitated traumas
that still haunt me

I've played with fire
ended up burnt
every bridge I
set aflame
believe a lesson
was learnt

lost in the madness
but found myself
along the way
my pains and perils
made me who I am today

The Rebuild

Antonio

I am at a point in my life where things or life should I say, are comming full circle. I call the past years of my life 1990-2013 the teardown. In that time I endured, bullets, knives, fists, boots, and bottles. All the while drinking while having a chronic illness that deteriorated my kidneys.

Now, I am living a new lifestyle. One of true healing. This part of my life I call the rebuild. I have put my demons to rest. Made peace with myself and to most I have wronged in the past. I help instead of hurt, and that heals.

The Rebuild

I am at a point in my life where things,
or life should I say, are coming full circle.
I call the past years of my life, 1990-2013,
The Teardown. In that time, I endured bullets,
knives, fists, boots and bottles. All the while
I was drinking while having a chronic illness
that deteriorated my kidneys.

Now I am living a new lifestyle. One of true
healing. This part of my life I call *The Rebuild*.
I have put my demons to rest. Made peace
with myself and to most I have wronged in
the past.

I help instead of hurt, and that heals.

Broke down feeling hollow (the first 48)

Broke down feeling hollow
looking blue
no clue what
I wanted to do
overwhelmed by adversity
swept away in
its tide
numb to worldly pain
dead on the inside
asking myself
is this what it's like
when thugs cry?
Cease this calamity
that has me
on the verge
of insanity
narcissistic tendencies
make my pain
my vanity
holographic smiles mask
peace of mind
on pause
like its buffering
hair-trigger
aggression
has my family
guessin'
my spiritual
direction
the man in
the mirror
is a bad reflection
under a veil

of darkness
that covers
like a shroud
all this anguish
has my demons
aroused
for the first
time in my life
I sensed fear
reaper whispering
in my ear
that he's near
using power of persuasion
he tried to seduce
"just fashion your shirt
into a noose,
do it quick
before someone comes,
give it a pull and
go numb"
almost convinced
with tears
in my eyes
then I realized
the devil is
a lie
untied my shirt
threw it to the
ground
made a promise
to turn my life
around
6 years later
Takin' on Life
is where I can
be found

Another cold night

Sunrise,
giving thanks
asking for help
remembering it is only
temporary
stale donated donuts and
cold coffee
constitute breakfast
off to the community center
for a morning shower
sunrise shame glows
illuminating streets,
sticking to back alleys
to stay out of public eye
I am the eyesore
society turns a blind
eye to
No begging, sign holding
or panhandling here
just optimism that
it will get better
despite multiple
rejections, still I try
employers not hiring
landlords not leasing
seeking refuge in
a dank dark
church basement
hanging my head

passing through
a soup line
belly full of hope
heart full of ambition
backpack full of
food pantry pickings
seeking a warm
place to stay
before sundown
so tired
so desperate
trying to avoid
another cold night
tucked in on cold concrete steps

forever scorned

Trying to slay
my demons
with a double-edged
sword
creating more trouble
than I can afford

sacrificial blood
for the greater
good
I haven't always done
quite as I should

far from a saint
more like a sinner
my demons are hungry
and the devil came
to dinner

angel on my left
devil on my right
a crown of thorns
couldn't conceal
my halo of thorns

seems I will be
forever scorned

Still trying to break free 2

Awake
regained consciousness
from major heart surgery
still groggy from the anesthesia
still in a dream state
what dream?
My reoccurring nightmare
of prison
so real so clear
fighting opps
in the yard
dream shattered
"Anthony calm down"
shouted by a nurse
as I swing
in the darkness
Damn, I just
can't break free

still trying to break free a
~~Swinging in the track a~~   Antonio S.O.

Awake
regained conciousness
from major heart surgery
still groggy from the
anestesia
still in a dream state
what dream?
my reaccurring nightmare
of prison.
So real so clear
fighting opps
on the yard
dream shattered
"Anthony calm down"
being shaked by
a nurse
as I swing
in the darkness
damn, I just
cant break free

Prompted (part 1)

Seems like yesterday
I was wrong again
down on luck
homeless, hungry,
hopelessly addicted
with a one-way
ticket back
to prison

13 years later
I can't believe
what my life
has become
clarity, peace of mind
and love
are at the center
of my daily existence
no more suppressed feelings
no hiding now
I stake myself
to the ground
and fight
I don't hold back
this isn't a movie

Of all my worldly possessions
that I will leave behind
when I expire
my written words

in a book
will cement my legacy
as I take a chance
and put my pain
out there
for the world
to see
like how I used
to roam into the night
breaking my one promise
to my mother

Or how
all my life
in my mind
I have been alone
with the sound
of this machine
in my head
that had me

Ceremony

Two prayer candles, one of the *Virgen de Guadeloupe,*
the other of *Santa Muerte,* flicker in the dark confines of
a closet. The altar on which they sit is made of a small
dresser draped with a black sequined veil. In the
center of the altar between the two candles is a plain
solid red candle melted down and pooled into a glass
dish at the base. In the pool of melted transparent
wax rests a sliver of paper that reads the name of
the individual for whom the spell is intended.

To the right of the melted candle is a sterling silver
Catholic-style crucifix. Fresh drops of blood are speckled
along its shiny surface, part of the sacrifice of the
ceremony
underway. To the left of the center candle
is a small brown owl feather, at the base of its black
beaded quill are three leather thongs. The scent of
burning dragon's blood drifts through the air, as the
smoke floats upwards. A shot glass of rum is placed
in front of the red candle. A sip is taken and
sprayed over all objects and a framed picture
depicting St. Michael's eviction from heaven into
the flames of Hell. A puff of a Cuban cigar and
an exhale of smoke blown over the altar with a
rosary clenched in a firm grasp, prayers are
murmured and I back away—my work is done.

rock and dirt

It is a brisk fall morning. The sunshine emits a warmth that contrasts with the morning breeze. The leaves on the trees are an assortment of orange, red and yellow. The smell of the fire is thick in the air, accompanied by the fragrance of cedar and sweetgrass. There's a slight tickle of a morning dew on my feet as I walk through the grass. The sound of the crackling fire heating the rocks for the ceremony breaks the silence of prayers and preparation. I make my round, around the lodge and stop at the altar. I say my prayer to *"Misho"* (creator) and give my tobacco offering. I walk down the fire path to the entrance of the lodge. On my knees I bow to the rock and dirt (mother earth) and pray for a spiritual cleansing. I enter the lodge, take my place on the northside. The scent of cedar fills my nostrils and I inhale deeply. As I exhale, I pray.

The first four rocks come in the lodge, each one creating a more intense heat. I can tell this is going to be a good sweat. Beads of perspiration have already formed. I'm ready to sacrifice, I'm ready to cleanse. The door is closed, and in the darkness the rocks glow a combination of red and orange. I am calm yet anxious, curious as to how hot this lodge will be, will I make it to the buffalo round? I will . . . I must. The sound of the first dipper of water is poured on the rocks, followed by the hiss of the boiling water. Then the sting of the steam pierces my body: *"mitake Oysin* . . . let us begin."

fogged in

I exhale smoke
as I reminisce
how things once were
and come to be like this

traveled to Hell and back
while keeping my mind intact
managed to see the light
when all faded to black

grey hairs show I've learned
scars show I've lived
ink in my skin depicts
my battles within
where angels and demons
both coincide
and the war that ensues
when they collide

shadows of my past
try to eclipse my future
as I attempt to hold it together
like a fresh suture

vines of vengeance
suffocate roots of love
asking for inner peace
one prayer, one smudge
clear my mind, body and soul
no longer being fogged in
is the goal

Lifeline

A pinch of the skin
a poke of the vein
a slight cold chill
a seeping sensation
throughout the body
as toxins are flushed out
and purities pumped in
functions of a normal kidney
now performed by a machine
that whirs, clicks,
beeps and buzzes
a dose of nausea
as equilibrium
is unbalanced
eyes heavy
drifting
drifting

I dance in the shadows of the moon

I dance in the shadows of the moon
and I fly too close to the sun
spent years chasing the ghost
in the web of addiction
I spun

graveyard in my closet,
exhumed memories
resuscitate traumas
that still haunt me

I've played with fire
and got burnt
every bridge I set aflame
believe a lesson was learnt

lost in the madness
but found myself
along the way
for the addict who still suffers
I still pray

one prayer one smudge
eliminating negative energy
align my chakras
and with my third eye I see

workday

3:30 comes early
house silent and warm
throw back the covers
let the heat escape
the morning is dark
and somber
shuffle to the bathroom
turn on the light
squint in the mirror
stubbles of grey
on the chin
dollop of toothpaste
dribble of water
from a whiney faucet
spit and rinse
wipe my face
with a hand towel
thrown crumpled
in a hamper
dressed and
headed upstairs
cold water in a
coffee pot
fresh filter
fresh grounds
it can't percolate
fast enough
two weeks straight
no days off

got to make quota
today
keeping my spot
on mixer #3
barely making pay
in the salad plant
that's 0 degrees and warmer
than it is outside
this morning

Turn the page

The story of
my life
is an
open book
pain and adversity
bind the pages
chapters of suffering
and sorrow

Chapter death,
watching my father die
at age twelve
watching my mother die
20 years later

Chapter darkness
13 years in a cell
entangled in a web
of addiction for 24 years

Chapter Redemption
with my writing
I created a legacy
of hope

Chapter lonely
craving companionship
despite how
hard a read
this book can be
I can always
turn the page

Antonio S.O.

Invictus

I've danced in the shadows of the moon
I have flown too close to the sun
I've ran with the devil
I flirted with death for fun
been grazed by a bullet
been sliced by a blade
all while enduring a chronic illness
most of my days
Spent my life makin my bones
now I just wanna rest them
by the fire
Call me "invictus"; unconquered
when I retire

Anto

in the shadows of the moon
have flown too close to the sun
I've ran with the devil
I flirted with death for fun
been grazed by a bullet
been sliced by a blade
all while enduring a chronic illness
most of my days
Spent my life makin my bones
now I just wanna rest them
by the fire
"invictus"; unconquered

V. Ending

when it's my time to go

I will be ready

I've been fighting this war within myself

I've been fighting this
war within myself
a lifelong battle
ensues
feeling at times
like my sanity
serves as
collateral damage
traumatized
thoughts
...ght terrors
...lusive tendencies
after effects
the conflict within
happiness,
and love
unfortunate
casualties

I write because
I write because...

I am somewhat introv...
with a dose of alexit...

write because...

...clutters my mind
...es the negativity
...pleneshes peace
...holding my demons

...e because....

...discovery
...tal freedom

...cause ...

testimony
...er of writi...

Antonio S.O.

A mile in my shoes   By Antonio

I had once seen an interview with Mr. T, where he
made a valid point and influenced me. In his interview
he wore his usual attire, sweat pants, a muscle tee, and
of course was adorned with several gold chains, to accom...
his trademark mohawk.

During the interview the reporter poked fun at his
shoes, some ragged sneakers. Mr. T's response to
the reporters comments was,"I wear them, because they
remind me of where I came from, before I got famous

Sweat Lodge (Part V)

One of the members outside the lodge covers the doorway in layers of blankets cutting off all sunlight into the lodge, making it pitch black. Engulfed by the darkness and embraced by the warmth, I sit.

The rocks in the pit glow red and as Kumali sprinkles cedar again on the rocks, the snapping and popping sound breaks the silence and again tiny flames are created and briefly illuminate the lodge, allowing me to see the silhouettes of the men.

My heart is beating a fast rhythm. I feel the first beads of sweat run down my face. My body is already covered in a layer of perspiration from the humidity. I hear the water in the bucket splash, and know what's next, the heat, the piercing sting of the steam as the water is poured on the rocks. The sound of the rapid beat of the drum starts as if to introduce the upcoming heat.

I hear the sound of the water in the bucket splash as Kumali scoops the dipper full of water. Everything is amplified and all my senses are heightened. I sit in extreme expectation of the unification of the water and rock.

A splash is followed by a roaring hiss as the water is poured. I can feel the steam rise to the top of the lodge and spread to the sides and slowly caress my back. My skin begins to feel the warmth, sweat continues to develop and cascade down my face and the rest of my body. Another explosive burst is heard and the heat intensifies.

Headaches and heartaches

Headaches and heartaches
go hand in hand
each leads to the other
and vice versa
it's the human condition

time to go
when it's my time to go
I will be ready
been a long time
  a lifetime of
preparation
  when it's my time to go
there will be no regrets
for I will be thankful I
had time to switch
things around

  the fame
it ain't what it's cracked up
to be
never got me
anything positive
except my writing
for which I am
known

The things I miss

The smell of spring rain
The cool breeze gently blowing on my skin
The sound of a lawnmower humming in the
   distance
Wet kisses from my pet dog
Sitting to watch the sun rise
Watching that same day's sun set
   in the west
Stomping in a puddle with a
   child-like innocence
The sound of a percolating coffee pot
The smell of a home-cooked breakfast
The laughter of my children
The company of a woman
Cruising in my car on a Sunday afternoon
The company of friends
The flakes of a winter's first snow

I miss my life

In my absence

In the event of my absence
I let it be known
I hold myself accountable
for all my choices and actions
I accept my imperfections and shortcomings
I admit and own my mistakes
I forgive
with no expectations
of any in return
I think of you daily
cry for you nightly
painfully accepting
this void

In my absence

In my absence
I owe you a deep apology
I apologize for the choices I made
that left you alone in this world
my irresponsible behavior is inexcusable

Not fair you suffer for my choices
and actions
void in my life
space in my heart
hoping you don't hate me
praying you accept me
accept my fate

You only know the person I was
not the man I've become
I've never got to call you son
I don't deserve to be called Dad

Shadows of my past

Shadows of my past
eclipse my future
repeated futile attempts
to step into the light
guilt is the handcuffs
regret is the belly chain and
fear shackles my feet,
bound for life.

they say forgiveness is the key
but I've yet to find it.
these scars remind me
of a painful past
every one a lesson learned

hell, I should have a doctorate degree
from the school of hard knocks
'cause I feel like I got tenure

How I'm feeling lately

How I'm feeling lately
ain't no tellin'
what lies beneath
a riddle box of
emotions
in a hall of mirrors
where death
deals the cards
and the reaper
has an ace
up his sleeve
you gamble
on the devil's
playground
house wins

This pen and paper

This pen and paper
is my salvation
words forged
in ink
soothing my spirit
thoughts congregate
as I decipher
the meaning
grasping dissected
thoughts
emotions birthed
from feelings
cascade onto paper
I trust this process
to break me through
the other side

Simple prayers

Morning water
cleanse my soul
wash away my sorrows
cedar smoke
carry my grief
up to the skies above
mother earth
absorb my tears
I am a pitiful
human being
thunder beings
carry my message
to my mother
and father
oh sacred fireplace
bless all my relatives

Worldly Possessions

I am not a wealthy man when it comes
to worldly possessions in the materialistic sense,
by society's standards. No, I don't claim a large
amount of land (can you really "own" the earth beneath
your feet?) to reside on, or even have a home for that
matter. I don't have a vast wardrobe of expensive
clothes (just what's on my back), or flashy jewelry
or designer fragrances. Nor do I own a fancy automobile.
(Hell, public transportation is considered a luxury to me).
I am a simple man, some would probably call me
boring. It's not to say I didn't have these items
at one point in my life, or possess the desire to
"live the good life." However, through my life's journey
I've learned to do without these things and remain
humble. (I have experienced homelessness and discovered
the blessings of a place to lay my head when I sleep
and a piece of bread).

So what I believe to be my worldly possessions
are as follows:
First are my memories, both the good and the bad,
those of joy and pain. All of which I own, no one can take
them from me. Some I wish to grasp
tightly because they make me happy, others I wish
to be banished for eternity. Nonetheless they are mine.
Second are my scars and tattoos. Both of which tell the story
of my 38 trips around the sun.
Finally, my lifelong "afflictions." The reason I name them so
is because I've been told that these "diseases" were given to

me genetically. I am plagued with alcoholism, diabetes and anger issues. I have fought a lifelong battle with these and will continue to do so until it's my time to walk on.

An elder once told me, "We own nothing, not even our bodies, we only have the use of our bodies until they wear out. Objects simply pass through our hands without permanence."

Taking my shot

I can't rid
my brain
of this pain
that's like a
boomerang
soon as I
chuck it
there it is again
no rest for
the wicked
can someone
fix it?
my thoughts
are explicit
my intentions
are pure
heart heavy
from adversity
endured
one prayer
one smudge
is all I got
they say
shoot for the moon so
I'm taking my shot

Tread lightly

As I tiptoe
down the corridors
of my mind
I tread lightly
on dead memories
cautious not
to rouse demons
from their slumber
wary to wake
the sleeping giant
walking a thin line
between a past
and present
headed towards
the light
stepping out of
the shadows
onto eggshells
hopscotching through
this landmine of
traumas
trying to stay
on my square
skating on thin ice
trying not to fall
through the cracks

4 in the morning

In the dark somber
still of the night
slumber interrupted
by a fragmented sentence
a simple phrase
settled in my subconscious
causes me to stir
in the twilight
rustling, fumbling to find paper
and pen to scribe
the perfect line to complete
the pestering puzzle
of a poem project or, wait,
was it a title?
or an opening line?
if the silence would only stop
ringing
I could concentrate.
What was it?
now a soft tap-tap
as rain
hits my windowsill
a rumble of thunder
and the taps
become amplified
the perfect line
washed away

Conviction

Eternal confliction
wears on my soul
searching for peace
among smiling faces
and transparent truths
with love in my heart
and blood on my hands
and conviction
in my heart

Antonio Sanchez-Day

1974 - 2021

Anthony J. Sanchez-Day, 46, of Lawrence, passed away on Friday, March 5, 2021, at the University of Kansas Medical Center in Kansas City, Kansas.

He was born July 21, 1974, in Topeka, the son of Frederick Sanchez and Delores M. Pimentel-Day. He graduated from Grand River Academy in Ashtabula, Ohio, and attended Haskell University for Liberal Arts.

Anthony was a freelance writer. His writings included poetry and short stories.

He was a member of the Prairie Band Potawatomi Nation. Anthony offered his creative writing skills by volunteering with inmate programs at the Douglas County Jail. His work with the inmate reentry program was his passion.

Anthony was preceded in death by his parents, Frederick and Delores.

Survivors include his step-father, Robert Day, Lawrence; a son, Ontario and a daughter, Ana; one brother, Robert Day, III, Lawrence; three aunts, Margaret Vasquez (Richard), and

Barbara Calvillo (Frank), all of Topeka, and Linda Leavitt (Jack), Lakewood Ranch, FL; one uncle, Blas Ortiz (Linda), Topeka; several cousins, including, Lisa Ortiz, Topeka, Sara Ortiz, Gabriel Ortiz (Jessica) and Christine Ortiz, all of Lawrence; a niece, Calli Day, and a nephew, Robert IV Day, both of Lawrence. Several friends in Anthony's life whom he considered his brothers as extended family.

photo by Greg Hellman

Antonio Sanchez-Day and Brian Daldorph

POETRY

Books are a way to explore, connect, and discover. Poetry incites us to observe and think in new ways, bridging our understanding of the world with our artistic need to interact with, shape, and share it with others.

Publishing poetry is our way of saying—

We love these words,
we want to preserve them,
we want to play a role in sharing them
with the world.

Follow Meadowlark Press on

Facebook & Instagram

facebook.com/ReadAMeadowlarkBook

Instagram @meadowlarkbooks

www.ingramcontent.com/pod-product-compliance
Lightning Source LLC
Chambersburg PA
CBHW061156120626
46546CB00005B/2089